A Job for Merv

Alison Prince

Illustrated by
David Higham

A Belitha Press Book

MARILYN MALIN BOOKS
in association with ANDRE DEUTSCH

Chapter 1

Merv roller-skated slowly down the street. Things were looking bad. All he had in the world were his roller skates and a personal stereo which played music to him through his earphones. He needed a job. And there weren't many jobs about.

Merv had worked at several places since he left school. He had been a white-line painter, touching up the white lines

down the middle of the road. But he'd got the sack for painting a big smiling face in the middle of the High Street. He had worked in a cake factory, squirting pink cream into sponges. But he'd got the sack for putting too much cream in, so that it squished all over the place. He had been a sticker-up of posters. But he'd got the sack for sticking them upside-down, because they looked funnier that way.

So now he needed a job.

He'd tried to be a dustman but the Council wouldn't have him. They hadn't forgotten about the face on the road.

He'd applied for a job in a pea factory, sorting brown peas from green ones, but the factory manager had heard about what he did with the cream. *He* wouldn't have him. In desperation, he had dyed his hair purple and tried to enrol as an art student, but the head of the art school said anyone who couldn't stick posters the right way up was obviously not artistic. So now Merv was skating slowly down the street, wondering what on earth he was to do next.

Then a notice attached to a spiky iron gate in front of a large house caught his

attention. In writing as spiky as the gate, it said *Man Wanted*. It looked as if it had been there for some time. The rain had run down the letters, leaving them faded and dribbly. Still, Merv thought, it was worth a try. After all, there weren't many jobs about.

He pushed the gate open and skated up the garden path to the flight of steps which led to the imposing front door. He crashed his way up these steps, sideways because of his roller skates, and rang the large brass bell. There was no answer, so he rang again.

The door was snatched open and a cross-looking woman stood there. 'Take your finger off my bell,' she said. 'I polished it this morning.'

'Sorry,' said Merv. He wondered if he should offer to polish his finger, but decided against it.

'You have left my gate open,' snapped the woman. 'And made nasty marks on my gravel path, and just *look* at the step. You are *standing* on it.'

'Yes,' Merv agreed meekly. 'I can't help it. If I was a helicopter, I'd hover. But I'm not.'

The woman took no notice. 'What do you want?' she demanded.

'I'm applying for the job,' said Merv. 'Like it says on the gate. *Man Wanted.*'

'Ah,' said the woman. She looked at Merv carefully. 'You are not my idea of a Man,' she said. 'You are more what I would call a Youth. Your hair is a very peculiar colour. And what is that thing on your chest? Are you deaf?'

'No,' said Merv. 'Only when I turn the music up too loud.'

'How very unpleasant,' said the woman. Her own hair was screwed into a bun on the top of her head, with lots of pins, and she clutched her cardigan across her chest suspiciously.

'What makes you think you are fitted for the post of Man?' she asked. 'Are you an experienced gardener?'

'No,' said Merv. 'But I'm handy.'

'Can you do carpentry, fix electricity,

stop draughts, mend anything I require you to mend and keep out unwanted visitors?' the woman enquired.

'I could try,' said Merv. 'And I *am* handy.'

'You don't sound handy to me,' said the woman severely.

Merv grinned. 'Oh, I am,' he assured her. 'Honest. I live just round the corner. Couldn't be handier.' Then he regretted it, because she looked more severe than ever. Perhaps she'd heard the joke before, he thought.

'Get off my step,' said the woman. 'Take those revolting things off your feet and go round to the back door, closing the side gate behind you. I will show you the sheds.' And she shut the door with a firm click.

Merv clumped down the steps and took his roller skates off. He took his personal stereo off, too, and stuffed it into his

pocket. Then he went through the side gate and shut it behind him obediently. This woman was terribly fierce, he thought – but he really *did* need a job.

'Sheds,' said the woman. 'Tool, wood and potting.' She waved a hand at what looked like a field of hay and added, 'The lawn needs cutting.'

'You could say that,' Merv agreed. He glanced at a bed of waist-high nettles and wondered whether the woman had grown them on purpose. They were the kind of plant she might like.

'Geraniums,' she said, following his gaze. 'They need weeding. You can do that when you've finished the lawn. When can you start?'

'Tomorrow,' said Merv. 'First thing. Say about eleven.'

'Eight o'clock, and not a moment later,' said the woman. 'I shall be waiting.'

Chapter 2

By skating very fast, Merv managed to arrive on time the next morning. He shut the front gate and the side gate behind him, and found his new employer standing by the sheds, looking at her watch.

'You were very nearly late,' she said. 'Don't let it become a habit. What is your name?'

'Merv,' said Merv. 'What's yours?'

'Pike,' said the woman. 'Agatha Pike. Miss. And I do not indulge in idle conversation. The mower is in the tool shed.' And she went back to the kitchen and shut the door.

The mower had been unused for so long that it wouldn't work, and it was covered with rust. Merv cleaned it and oiled it, put some petrol in it and at last persuaded it to start, then tackled the hay. It was very hard work. He had to take his skates off because they got tangled in the grass, and the mower was so noisy that he could hardly hear the music in his earphones.

After three hours he went and tapped on the kitchen door.

'Yes?' enquired Miss Pike, opening it.
'Tea-break,' said Merv.
Miss Pike stared at him. 'I beg your pardon?' she said.

'Tea-break,' Merv repeated. 'You know – sit down, weight off the feet, cup of tea.'

For a moment, he thought she was going to slam the door. Then she said crossly, 'You'd better come in.'

'Thank you,' said Merv.

He washed his hands at the sink, watching Miss Pike out of the corner of his eye while she put the kettle on. Nobody had done any work around the place for a long time, he thought, otherwise the garden wouldn't be so overgrown and the mower so rusty. Perhaps Miss Pike found it difficult to get a Man to stay. It wasn't surprising, with her being so cross all the time. 'Got a towel?' he asked.

'The brown one,' said Miss Pike. 'Hang it up afterwards. And take your shoes off – they are making green marks on my floor.'

Merv hung up the towel, then sat down and pulled off his shabby old trainers. A lot of grass clippings fell out, and there was a hole in his sock.

Miss Pike closed her eyes and said faintly, 'You had better put them on again.'

'Might be an idea,' Merv agreed.

There was an uneasy silence while the kettle boiled and Miss Pike made the tea. She placed a cup before him, tight-lipped.

'Sugar?' asked Merv.

Miss Pike glared at him, but produced a tin marked Sugar and tipped some into a glass bowl with a silver spoon in it.

'Got any bikkies?' Merv asked hopefully.

Miss Pike's eyes bulged. But she snatched open a cupboard and got out a biscuit barrel which she banged down on the table.

'Ta,' said Merv. He took a biscuit and dunked it in his tea. 'Must be a long time since anyone cut your lawn,' he said. 'It's waist-high.'

Miss Pike was still standing by the table, one hand on the back of the chair, the other clutching her cardigan. 'They don't stay,' she said suddenly. 'Men.

They come, work for a day or two, then off they go. They're all the same. I expect you will be, too. Take your elbows off the table!' she added fiercely. 'Have you no manners?'

'It's ever so comfortable like this,' said Merv, not moving. 'You ought to try it.'

'Don't be impertinent,' said Miss Pike, and pushed a couple of pins back into her hair. She fetched herself a cup and saucer and poured herself a cup of tea, but she did not sit down.

Merv thought about the rain-washed notice on the gate and the long uncut grass. Most probably, word had got round that Miss Pike was impossible to work for. So nobody would apply for the job. He, Merv, was the only Man she was likely to get. But then, this job was the only one that *Merv* was likely to get. He drank his tea thoughtfully, then stood up and said, 'Thanks a lot.'

Miss Pike gave him a curt nod, and Merv went out to get on with the grass.

That afternoon he gave himself another tea-break.

'Wipe your feet,' said Miss Pike. But she already had the kettle on.

'Okay,' said Merv. When he thought he had wiped enough, he washed his hands and dried them on the brown towel and hung it up. Then he sat down at the table and said, 'It must get lonely here, all by yourself.'

'Mind your own business,' snapped Miss Pike.

'Okay,' said Merv again.

Chapter 3

He finished the grass that afternoon, and made a start on the nettles. He turned up at eight o'clock the next morning and got on with them. When he went in for his tea-break, three neat envelopes lay on the table beside the biscuit barrel.

'I should be glad if you will post those on your way home,' said Miss Pike, nodding at the envelopes as she poured out Merv's tea. 'I have invited some people to a small gathering on Sunday afternoon.'

'That's nice,' said Merv. 'I don't like to think of you being lonely.'

Miss Pike pursed her lips but said nothing. She poured herself a cup of tea and sat down at the opposite side of the table, as far away from Merv as possible. Merv picked up the letters and glanced at them.

'Don't *finger* those!' said Miss Pike irritably. 'I will put them in a plastic bag for you to carry to the post.'

'Okay,' said Merv. The invitations, he had noticed, were to Mr Snodgrass, Solicitor, to Mr Pembleton, Bank Manager, and to Mr Quegg of Quegg, Burk and Whinnett, Accountants. Poor old thing, Merv thought. Didn't she have any proper friends? It sounded as if she was going to have a terribly dull party.

Merv posted the invitations on his way home for lunch. In the afternoon, he came back and got on with the nettles. Miss Pike watched him suspiciously through the kitchen window. This job wouldn't last long, Merv thought. Nobody stayed long with Miss Pike. It was a pity, really, because he quite liked it here. Working in the garden was much more fun than repainting white lines, or sticking up posters, or squirting pink cream into sponges.

Something flitted across the garden wall and landed on Merv's newly cut grass. It was, he saw, a paper dart. The kitchen window was flung open at once.

'Merv!' Miss Pike shouted. 'Come here!'

Merv did as he was told.

'It's those children from next door,' Miss Pike said angrily. 'They throw these disgusting things into my garden just to annoy me. Go and tell them not to do it again. Be firm.'

'Okay,' said Merv.

He picked up the paper dart and wandered across to the wall. He could hear giggling from the other side. He stood on the wheelbarrow and looked over. Four children were busy making paper darts.

'Hello,' said Merv. 'Here's your dart back.' He whizzed it down to them. He wondered how to be firm. 'She doesn't much like darts in her garden,' he said. 'Because she's having a party on Sunday and she wants it to be nice and tidy.'

'A party!' said the children excitedly. 'Ooh! Can we come?'

Merv hesitated. He looked at the children's delighted faces. This job

wouldn't last long, he told himself. Sooner or later, Miss Pike would give him the sack. So why not enjoy it while he could? He smiled at the children. 'Yes,' he said. 'Of course you can come. And your mum and dad as well. Only keep the darts out of Miss Pike's garden, okay?'

'Okay!' said the children happily, and dashed into the house to tell their mother about the party.

At tea-break that afternoon, Miss Pike said, 'I hope you were firm.'

'Well,' said Merv evasively, 'there haven't been any more darts.'

'So I noticed,' said Miss Pike. She looked almost pleased.

A dog barked outside. Miss Pike frowned again. 'That woman is always allowing her dog to bark,' she said. 'She does it on purpose. You had better go and deal with her. Be firm.'

'Can I finish my tea first?' asked Merv hopefully. He thought that by the time he had finished his tea, the barking dog and its owner would have gone away by themselves.

'No,' snapped Miss Pike. 'Deal with her now, while she is still there, you stupid boy.'

Reluctantly, Merv went out.

'Hello,' said the lady with the barking dog, which was wagging its tail at the same time. 'Are you Miss Pike's new Man?'

'Yes,' said Merv.

'The best of luck to you!' said the

woman. 'She's the most disagreeable, sour-faced old bat I've ever seen.'

'Oh, I don't know,' said Merv mildly. 'She's having a party on Sunday. The children next door are coming.'

'Really?' The woman was astonished.

'Perhaps I misjudged her. Can Bonzo and I come as well? We'll bring our own bones and things.'

'Why not?' said Merv recklessly. Miss Pike would probably give him the sack when she found out about the children next door, so one more wouldn't matter. He made a mental note to tell the children to bring their own jellies and pop. The woman with the dog went on down the street, smiling, and Merv went back and finished his tea.

Chapter 4

He arrived early the next morning, determined to be very sensible and not to invite any more odd people to Miss Pike's party. It was a wet, miserable day and he was surprised to find Miss Pike angrily shampooing the doorstep.

'That wretched milkman has climbed right up my steps with muddy feet!' she said when she saw Merv. 'I have told him again and again that when it is raining he is to bring the milk round to the back door, and mind he shuts the gate. But he takes no notice. Merv, I want you to call at the dairy on your way home and complain. Be firm.'

'I'll try,' said Merv. But his heart sank.

The dairy was full of cheerful milkmen whistling and crashing crates of bottles about. Merv found the man in charge and explained that he came from Miss Pike.

'That dismal old baggage!' exclaimed the man. 'I bet she's complaining again, isn't she?' He did not wait for Merv to

answer. 'Nobody can stand that woman,' he said. 'She's got no friends, and serve her right.'

'She *is* having a party,' Merv pointed out. 'On Sunday afternoon.'

'Not for milkmen, she isn't,' he said.

Merv forgot about being sensible. 'You could come,' he said. 'Everybody needs friends. That's what the party's for. But you'd better bring some milk, or there might not be enough.'

'We might just do that,' said the man. 'Give her a shock.'

'Do,' said Merv. And he went home for lunch, trying not to panic. He really had not meant to ask anyone else to the party.

At three o'clock that afternoon, Miss Pike came out of her front door and said, 'I am glad you were firm this morning. You may come into the kitchen for your tea-break. It is slightly early, but I wish to speak to you.'

Merv gulped. Had she found out what he had been up to? But, as he sat down for his cup of tea, Miss Pike said, 'I imagine, Merv, that you know about food.'

'Food?' queried Merv, taking a biscuit.

'Party food,' Miss Pike explained. A slight blush crossed her face. 'In actual fact,' she said, 'this is the first time I have invited people to the house for – er – quite some years.'

'Go on,' said Merv, taking another biscuit. 'I bet it's the first time ever.'

Miss Pike frowned. Then she said, 'Yes.

Well. But one must move with the times, Merv.' She put her cup of tea down on the table and drew up a chair. 'I wish to know,' she said, 'what visitors expect.'

'Well,' said Merv guiltily, 'when it comes to food, the main thing is to have plenty. There might be more people than you think.'

'There will be three,' said Miss Pike precisely. 'Four, including myself.'

Merv could not bring himself to tell her that it would be nearer fourteen than four. 'If you like,' he said, 'I'll come on Sunday morning and help you cut sandwiches and things. Not for wages, I mean. Just to help.'

To his amazement, Miss Pike's face cracked into a rusty smile. 'In that case, you may come to my party as well,' she said. 'That will make five. The more the merrier, as they say.'

'So they do,' said Merv. But he found it difficult to smile back.

Chapter 5

Merv skated off to Miss Pike's house on Sunday morning, feeling more guilty than ever. Since his conversation with her about the food, he had found himself inviting the postman, the coalman, the lady who came to sanitise the telephone, a girl collecting for Save the Whale, and four Boy Scouts.

Miss Pike was in a great state of nervousness about the thought of having three strangers in her house, and made huge numbers of neat little cakes in paper cases, while Merv cut piles and piles of sandwiches. 'It's a lovely day,' he said when he had finished. 'Shall I put the table outside? There'll be more room.'

'Is that usual?' enquired Miss Pike.

'Oh, absolutely,' Merv assured her.

'Very well, then,' she said, and went upstairs to change.

Merv arranged everything in the garden. Then, with the help of a friend called Tricky Harris, he rigged up a tape

recorder and loudspeakers, and put some lights in the trees. Then he asked Tricky Harris to come to the party, and Tricky said he'd love to. And he would bring his girl friend, Debbie, and her flat-mate, Fatima.

To Merv's immense relief, the first person to arrive was one of Miss Pike's invited guests, a man in a pin-striped suit.

'Ah, Mr Snodgrass!' said Miss Pike. 'Do come into the garden.'

'Pembleton, actually,' said the man, and gazed in some amazement at the lights and loudspeakers in the trees. 'Goodness,' he said. 'How very – er – up to date.'

Then the front door bell rang again. 'Merv – door,' said Miss Pike, smiling glassily at Mr Pembleton.

Merv went. There were about thirty people cramming themselves onto the

doorstep. The children from next door were jumping up and down with balloons and their parents were laden with jellies and pop. Several milkmen clutched crates of milk and pots of yogurt and parcels of melting ice-cream, and Bonzo held a huge bone. The postman brought sausage rolls and the Boy Scouts had dry sticks to make a bonfire and a huge bowl of something they called Damper Mixture, and the woman who sanitised telephones had sesame seed crunch. After that, Merv lost count as people surged past him, pushing their various offerings into his arms as

they went. He staggered after them into the garden where Miss Pike was staring in speechless horror at the invasion, and announced in a loud, cheerful voice, 'Surprise party!'

'Oh, frightfully smart,' said Mr Pembleton, looking happier. He turned to Miss Pike and added, 'Tell you the truth, dear lady, I did fear I'd find nothing but the same old crashing bores here – Snodgrass and Quegg, people like that. Ah, hello, Quegg!'

Merv, in his confusion, left the front door open. More people poured in.

It was an amazing party. The Boy Scouts lit a huge bonfire down by the compost heap and Bonzo's owner gave them lots of potatoes to bake in it. Music rang out from the speakers in the trees and as the sun went down, Tricky Harris switched on his lights and everyone danced. Mr Pembleton danced with Fatima and the coalman danced with the Save the Whale girl, and the children danced with everyone or all by themselves. After a while Miss Pike came over to Merv, who was experimenting with toasting ice-cream over the bonfire, wrapped in Damper Mixture. 'Take those roller skates off,' she instructed.

'Okay,' said Merv sadly. He stood up and gave his ice-cream to Bonzo, then took his skates off. This was the end, he thought. He was about to get the sack. Still, it had been fun while it lasted.

Miss Pike held up her arms, a little uncertainly. 'Merv,' she said, 'dance.'

'Whew!' said Merv as he swept her into some sort of tango across the new-mown lawn. 'You mean you don't mind about the party?'

'Mind?' said Miss Pike. 'Why should I mind?'

Miss Pike looked up at him in the radiance of Tricky Harris's lights. 'This is – *usual,* isn't it?' she asked. 'To have all these people arrive at your party.'

'Not *absolutely* usual,' Merv confessed. 'They came along because – because they want to be your friends. They all think you're wonderful.'

'Yes,' said Miss Pike a little bit complacently. 'They do. It seems that I have a talent for entertaining. I can't think why I didn't realise it before. I shall invite them again. Probably quite soon.'

When the music ended, Merv led Miss Pike back to the table amid applause. She sat down and eyed him severely. 'Mind you,' she said, 'just because I have allowed you to attend my party, Merv, I shall not expect the excitement to go to your head. You will arrive at eight o'clock tomorrow morning as usual, to weed the gravel path – not later.'

Tricky Harris and a couple of milkmen grinned when they heard this, but Merv didn't mind. After all, there weren't many jobs about. He smiled at Miss Pike and helped himself to a sausage roll. 'Okay,' he said.

First published in Great Britain in 1986 by
Marilyn Malin Books in association with André Deutsch Ltd.
105 Great Russell Street, London WC1B 3LJ

Conceived, designed and produced by Belitha Press Ltd.
2 Beresford Terrace, London N5 2DH

Copyright in this format © Belitha Press 1986
Text copyright © Alison Prince 1986
Illustrations copyright © David Higham 1986
Series design by Peter Wingham

All rights reserved. No part of this publication may be
reproduced in any form or by any means whatsoever without
permission in writing of the publishers
and the copyright holders.
10 9 8 7 6 5 4 3 2 1

ISBN 0 233 97947 6
Printed in Spain